Pachelbel's "Loose" Canon

arranged for four guitars

by The Los Angeles Guitar Quartet

John Dearman, William Kanengiser, Scott Tennant and Andrew York

Online PDF www.melbay.com/21756EB

To view a live performance of Pachelbel's "Loose Canon" performed by LAGQ please visit the following link:
http://www.youtube.com/watch?v=yflWG-e38OU

I0806892

1 2 3 4 5 6 7 8 9 0

Visit us on the Web at www.melbay.com — E-mail us at email@melbay.com

Notes on the Arrangement

Sometimes, boredom can be the best motivator. In Spring 1996, LAGQ was on tour in Japan, stuck in the Ginza Dai-ichi Hotel for three days during a torrential monsoon. Looming in their calendar was a recording of an all-Baroque CD for Delos Records (the oddly-titled "For Thy Pleasure"). Most of the repertoire for the disc had already been chosen, but the producer had practically begged for an arrangement of that "greatest hit" of all Baroque greatest hits, the Pachelbel Canon. Sitting in a stuffy boardroom, LAGQ started seriously fleshing out a traditional arrangement, but before long musical chaos took over. The groove shifted from classical to Reggae, then jazz, then punk, and before long the concept of this "Loose Canon" arrangement was born. Intended with the greatest respect to Herr Pachelbel, the re-imagining of his timeless composition in various pop styles is more of a indictment of the over-saturation of this clever canon in weddings, new-age recordings, and classical crossover CDs. To keep a small measure of integrity to an otherwise suspect setting of such a beloved piece, LAGQ incorporated some canonic imitation, albeit in salsa and rumba grooves.

When the present arrangement was presented to the aforementioned producer, her enthusiasm for it was so muted that the piece was only included as a "bonus track", (preceded by a 20 second pause to decrease the chances of it being heard!). Nonetheless, the arrangement worked its way into LAGQ programs as a tongue-in-cheek satirical encore, and ultimately became one of its most popular selections. After being featured on Mel Bay's "LAGQ Live at the Sheldon" (http://www.melbay.com/product.asp?ProductID=21047DVD), the piece went viral on Youtube, with over 1.5 million hits. Somewhat belatedly (that is, 16 years later) LAGQ is releasing the official published version by popular demand.

This arrangement is somewhat unique in the canon of LAGQ adaptations; it's the only one that is a true "group arrangement", rather than a project primarily crafted by an individual member. Because of the popular nature of some of the figuration, much of it was never written down, and frequently was subject to on-the-spot improvisation. But since a published version has to be somewhat definitive, this publication is mostly based on the DVD version, with a few details drawn from a more "ideal" rendition. The issue of John Dearman's 7-string guitar also poses some challenges, as it is assumed that many groups don't have access to such an instrument. With that in mind, Part 3 was adapted for standard 6-string guitar, with lower-octave indications (8vb) inserted where appropriate if played on 7-string.

While the piece is arranged for four classical guitars, the arrangement presumes a familiarity with popular styles and non-traditional techniques. Although some pains have been taken to indicate the nuances of the various styles, players are encouraged to familiarize themselves with source-recordings of the styles indicated, as well as the LAGQ performance itself. Some of the strumming patterns, especially the "funk" groove in Part 4 (mm. 101-114) and the "rumba" pattern (Parts 2 & 4, mm. 148-end) are quite idiosyncratic, and can be modified to fit the abilities of the player. What matters most is rhythmic feel and stylistic authenticity. Those players most adept at flamenco, percussion technique or bluegrass might take part 2, to handle the challenges of Scott Tennant's part. Those with a very strong bass range might take Part 3, to fill out the low register of John Dearman's guitar (and if a 7-string is available, certainly play this part). And those able to improvise in the jazz style, or at least swing a written-out solo, should play part 4. Just for fun, a written-out solo for the Jazz section is provided by Andy York, as well as an alternate solo improvised by current LAGQ member Matt Greif.

William Kanengiser

Pachelbel's "Loose" Canon

Johann Pachelbel (1653-1706)
"Loosely" arranged by the Los Angeles Guitar Quartet

molto rit.
poco cresc.
Reggae
♩ = 136
fleshy thumb ála electric bass
simile
fast downward strums
ponticello, metallico

36
ponticello, metallico
41
46

Tumbao
♩=112
slap on side or top of guitar: high conga sound
tap on top near bridge: low conga sound
percussion: damp strings w/left hand
tap on strings near bridge
tap on strings over fretboard
CIII

60
62
f
3
mf
(ad lib. fill)
65

Bluegrass
=112 slight swing feel
bright and accented; w/ plectrum if possible
prepare capo on 7th fret
"country" strum like banjo frailing pattern
simile
rhythm ad lib
bright and accented; w/ plectrum if possible

79
84
89
♩= 126
banjo imitation;
let notes ring
(sounds a 5th higher than notated)

93
fleshy thumb imitating
bluegrass bass; slap on rests ad lib
quick strum
97
percussion ad lib: slap strings against frets, muted strings
simile
101

Disco
♩ = 94
104
left hand slap on strings over fretboard
remove capo
right hand golpe on strings near bridge
Funk bass style
(8vb)
107
bend
bend
vib.
choke stroke
vib.
pluck w/downward stroke of index, as if holding a pick.
Create rock guitar harmonic "click" when possible
(8vb)
funk strum ad lib.
choke stroke
109
(8vb)

111
113
115
vib.
vib.
vib.
(8vb)
(8vb)
(8vb)

117
(8vb)
Jazz
♩= 168 swing
119
mp
light jazz comp feel
mp
fleshy jazz double-bass sound
DMaj7
A7(b13)
Bm9
F#7(b13)
Andy's solo
mf
Matt's optional solo; or improvise ad lib over changes
123
GMaj7
A13(b9)
GMaj6
A7(b13)

127
lightly tap or strum muted strings, snare imitation
DMaj7
A7(b13)
Fm7
Bb7(b13)
GMaj7
A13(b9)
132
DMaj7
GMaj6
A7(b9)
DMaj7
136
A7(b13)
DMaj7
F#7(b13)
GMaj7
DMaj7

141
Grunge
♩ = 120
GMaj6
A13(♭9)
GMaj6
A13(♭9)
144
Pa-chel- bel!!
scream in grunge guttural style
Pa-chel- bel!!
scream in grunge guttural style
Pa-chel- bel!!
scream in grunge guttural style
Pa-chel- bel!!
improvise wildly, using notes above fretboard
scream in grunge guttural style
147
continue to improvise freely and wildy, utilizing glisses

149
mf
Rumba
152
♩=200+
(slap on strings w/palm)
simile
strum in rumba style
tune ⑥ to E
158
f

163
molto staccato, sempre apoyando; "Gipsy Kings" style
168
173
(slap on strings w/ palm)
strum in rumba style
simile
178

183
188
193
198

203
208
(optional strum pattern)
213

218
cresc.
cresc.
cresc.
cresc.
223
226
ff
ff
ff
ff

Guitar 1

Pachelbel's "Loose" Canon

arranged for four guitars
by The Los Angeles Guitar Quartet

Standard Notation and Tablature

1 2 3 4 5 6 7 8 9 0

Visit us on the Web at www.melbay.com — E-mail us at email@melbay.com

Standard Notation

Pachelbel's "Loose Canon"

Guitar 1

Johann Pachelbel (1653-1706)
"Loosely" arranged by the Los Angeles Guitar Quartet

Bluegrass
𝅗𝅥 = 112 slight swing feel
bright and accented; w/plectrum if possible
♩ = 126
fleshy thumb imitating
bluegrass bass; slap on rests ad lib
Disco
♩ = 94
bend
bend
vib.
choke
stroke
vib.
pluck w/downward stroke of index, as if holding a pick.
Create rock guitar harmonic "click" when possible

vib.
vib.
vib.
Jazz
♩ = 168 swing
mp light jazz comp feel
Grunge
♩ = 120
ff
Pa-chel- bel!!
scream in grunge guttural style
Rumba
♩ = 200+

molto staccato, sempre apoyando;
"Gipsy Kings" style
a m i
f
cresc.
ff

Tablature

Pachelbel's "Loose" Canon

Guitar 1

Johann Pachelbel (1653-1706)
"Loosely" arranged by the Los Angeles Guitar Quartet

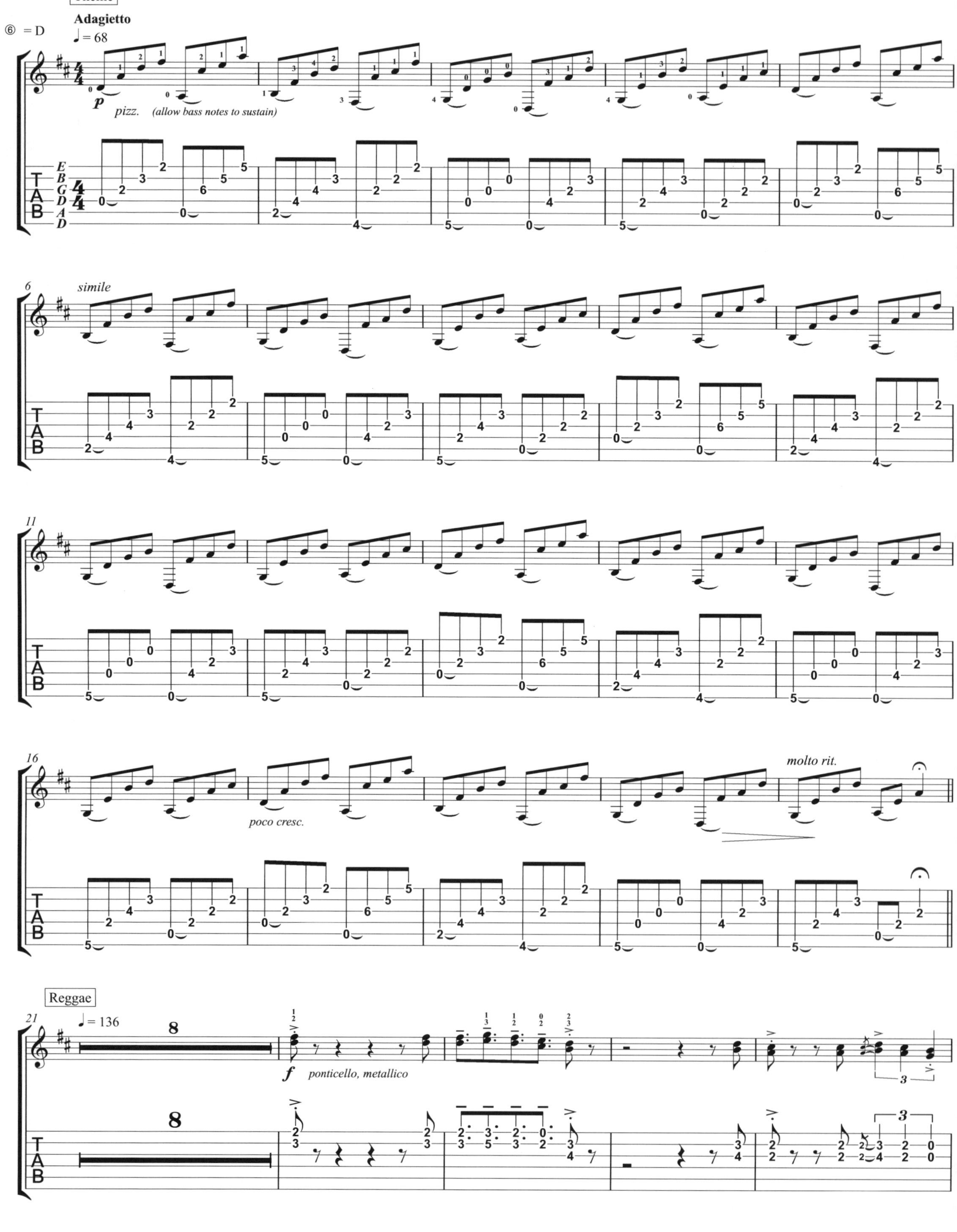

Tumbao
♩ = 112
ff
f

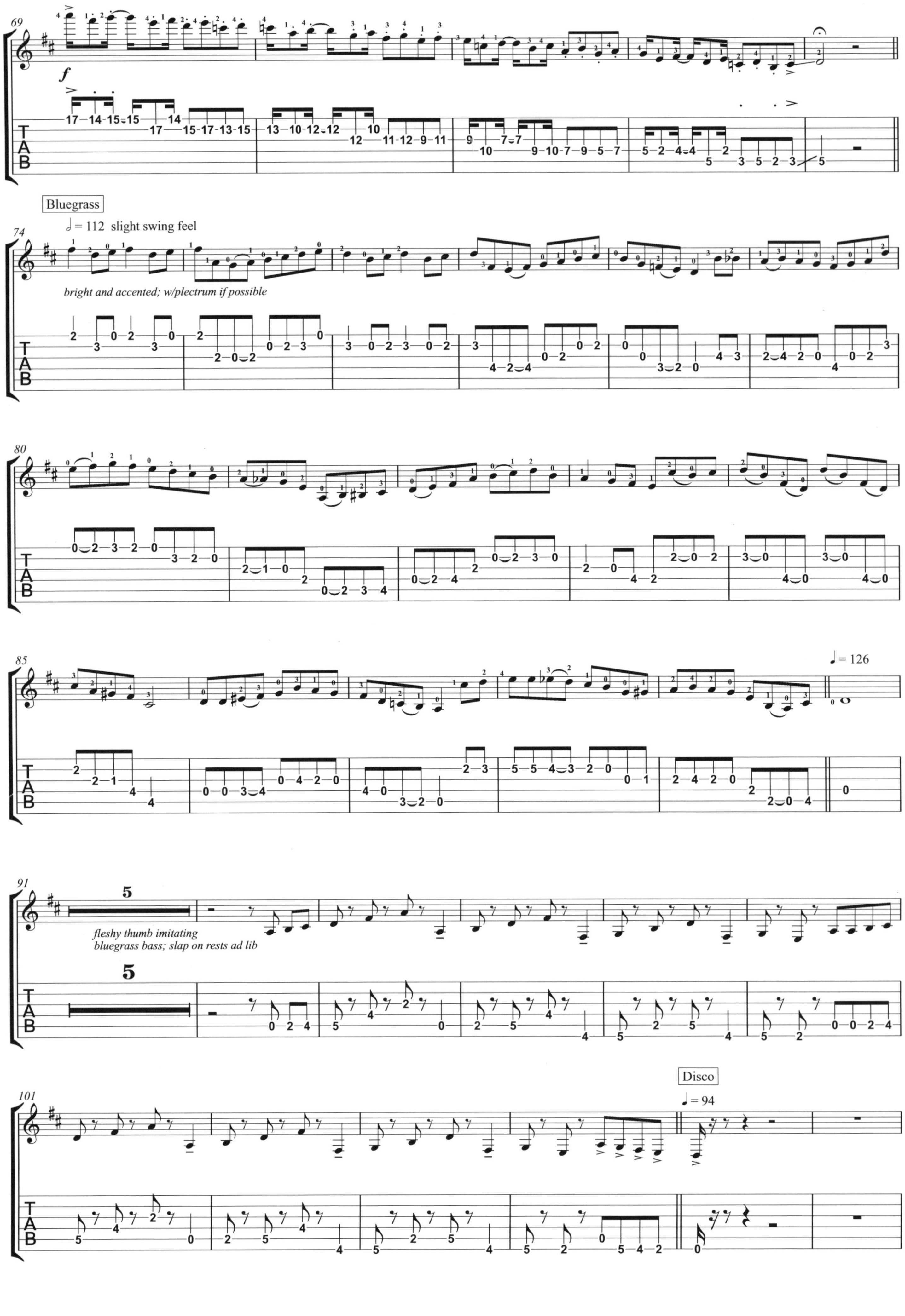
Bluegrass
= 112 slight swing feel
bright and accented; w/plectrum if possible
= 126
fleshy thumb imitating
bluegrass bass; slap on rests ad lib
Disco
= 94

bend
choke stroke
vib.
pluck w/downward stroke of index, as if holding a pick.
Create rock guitar harmonic "click" when possible
Jazz
♩= 168 swing
mp light jazz comp feel
GMaj7 A13(♭9) DMaj7
DMaj7 A7(♭13) Fm7 B♭7(♭13) GMaj7 A13(♭9) DMaj7

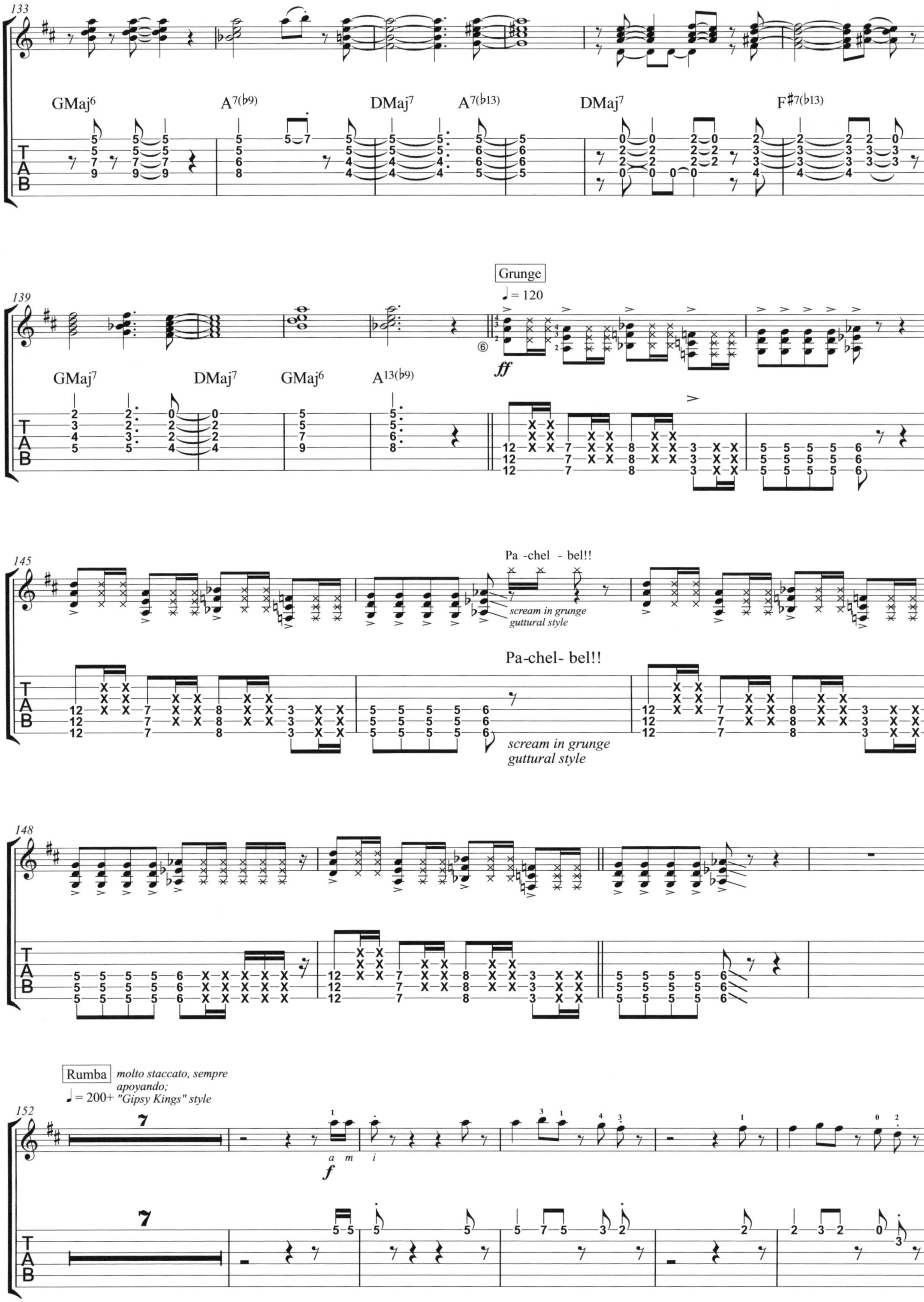
133
GMaj6
A7(♭9)
DMaj7
A7(♭13)
DMaj7
F♯7(♭13)
139
GMaj7
DMaj7
GMaj6
A13(♭9)
Grunge
♩ = 120
ff
145
Pa -chel - bel!!
scream in grunge guttural style
Pa-chel- bel!!
scream in grunge guttural style
148
Rumba
molto staccato, sempre apoyando;
♩ = 200+ "Gipsy Kings" style
152
f

164
170
176
182
187
192

cresc.
ff

MEL BAY®

Guitar Two

Pachelbel's "Loose" Canon

arranged for four guitars
by The Los Angeles Guitar Quartet

Standard Notation and Tablature

1 2 3 4 5 6 7 8 9 0

Visit us on the Web at www.melbay.com — E-mail us at email@melbay.com

Standard Notation

Pachelbel's "Loose" Canon

Guitar 2

Johann Pachelbel (1653-1706)
"Loosely" arranged by the Los Angeles Guitar Quartet

Tumbao
=112
slap on side or top of guitar: high conga sound
tap on top near bridge: low conga sound
percussion: damp strings w/left hand
tap on strings over fretboard
tap on strings near bridge
(ad lib. fill)
Bluegrass
=112 slight swing feel
prepare capo on 7th fret
banjo imitation; let notes ring
= 126
(sounds a 5th higher than notated)

Disco
♩= 94
left hand slap on strings over fretboard
remove capo
right hand golpe on strings near bridge
Jazz
♩= 168 swing
lightly tap or strum muted strings, snare imitation
Grunge
♩= 120

Pa-chel- bel!!
scream in grunge guttural style
Rumba
♩ = 200+
(slap on strings w/palm)
simile
strum in rumba style

189
194
199
204
209
214
219
cresc.
224
227
ff
3
3
3

Tablature

Pachelbel's "Loose" Canon

Guitar 2

Johann Pachelbel (1653-1706)
"Loosely" arranged by the Los Angeles Guitar Quartet

Tumbao
♩=112
slap on side or top of guitar: high conga sound
tap on top near bridge: low conga sound
ff
percussion: damp strings w/left hand
tap on strings over fretboard
mf
tap on strings near bridge

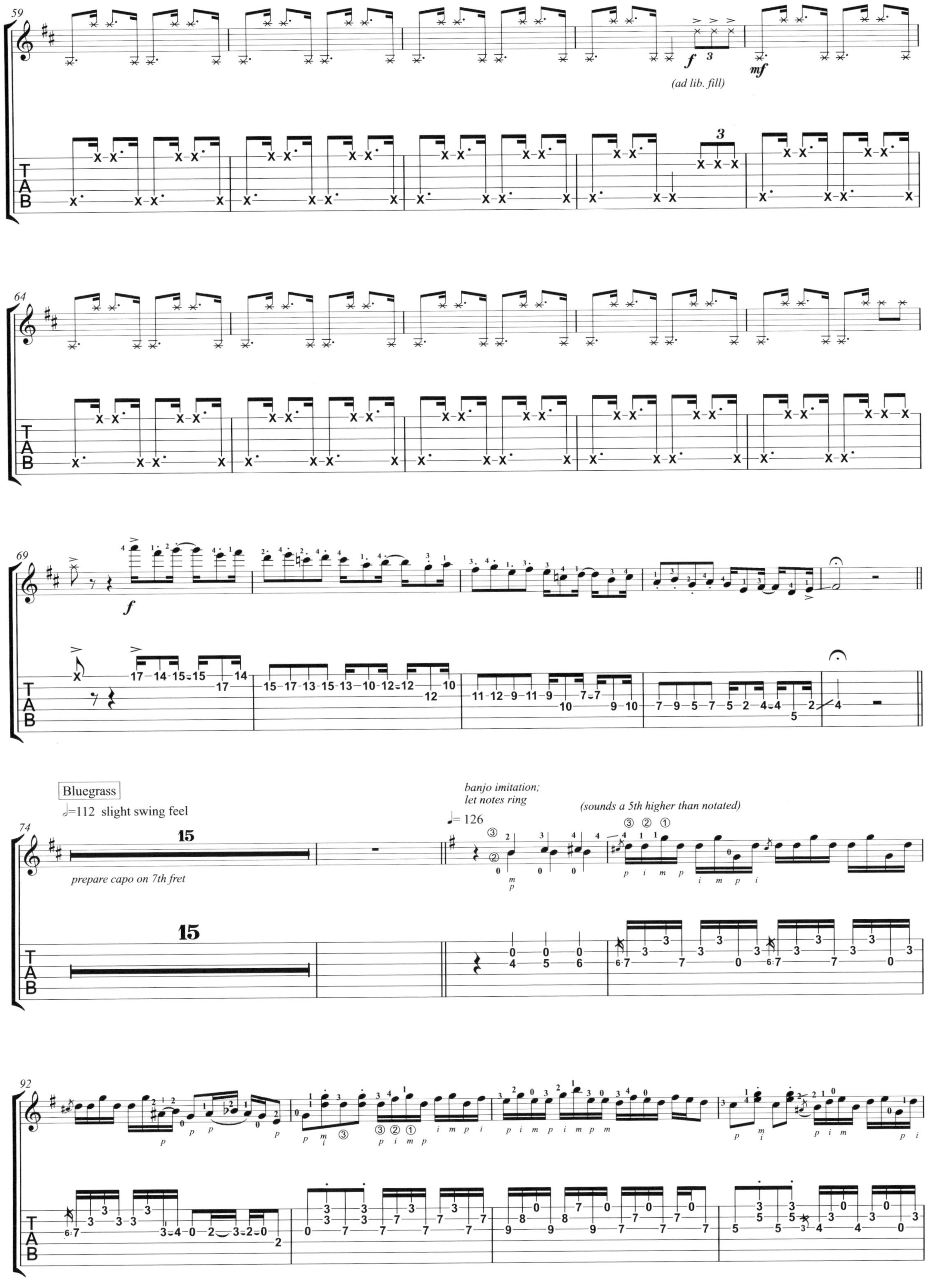
(ad lib. fill)
Bluegrass
𝅗𝅥=112 slight swing feel
prepare capo on 7th fret
banjo imitation;
let notes ring
♩= 126
(sounds a 5th higher than notated)

96
p i m
p i p i m
100
p m i
103
Disco
♩= 94
105
remove capo
left hand slap on strings over fretboard
right hand golpe on strings near bridge
109
113

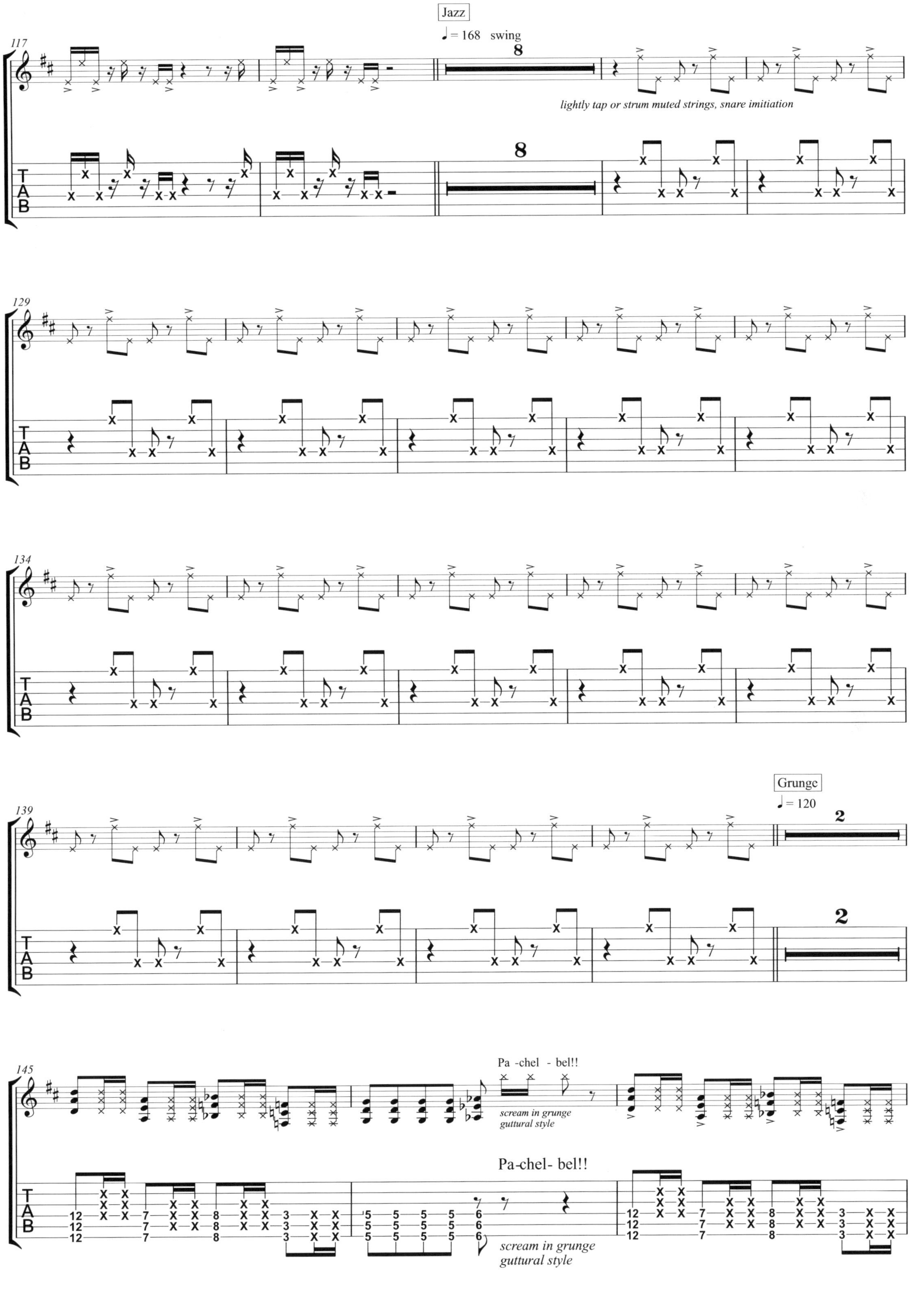
Jazz
♩ = 168 swing
lightly tap or strum muted strings, snare imitiation
Grunge
♩ = 120
Pa -chel - bel!!
scream in grunge guttural style
Pa-chel- bel!!
scream in grunge guttural style

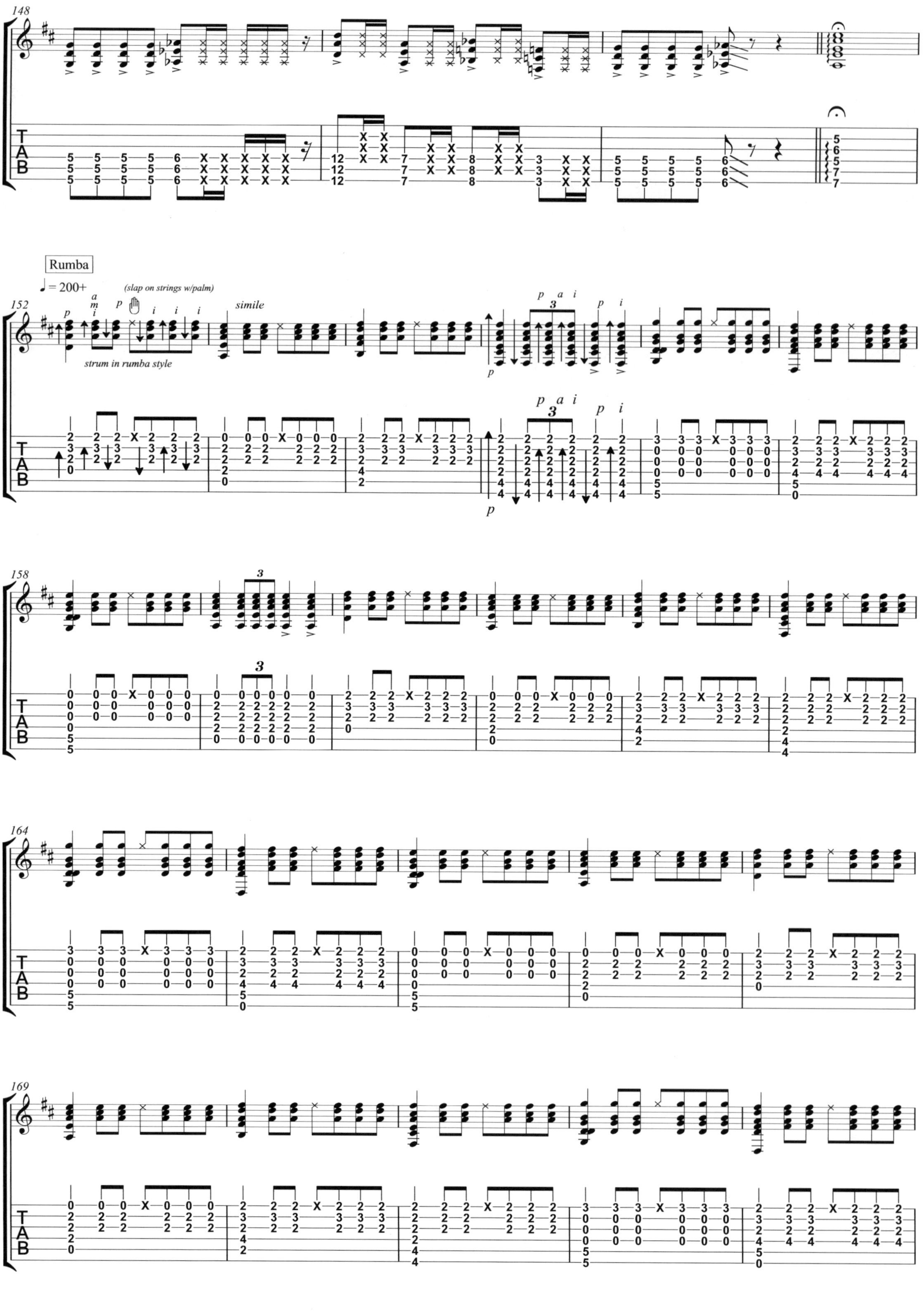
Rumba
♩ = 200+
(slap on strings w/palm)
simile
strum in rumba style

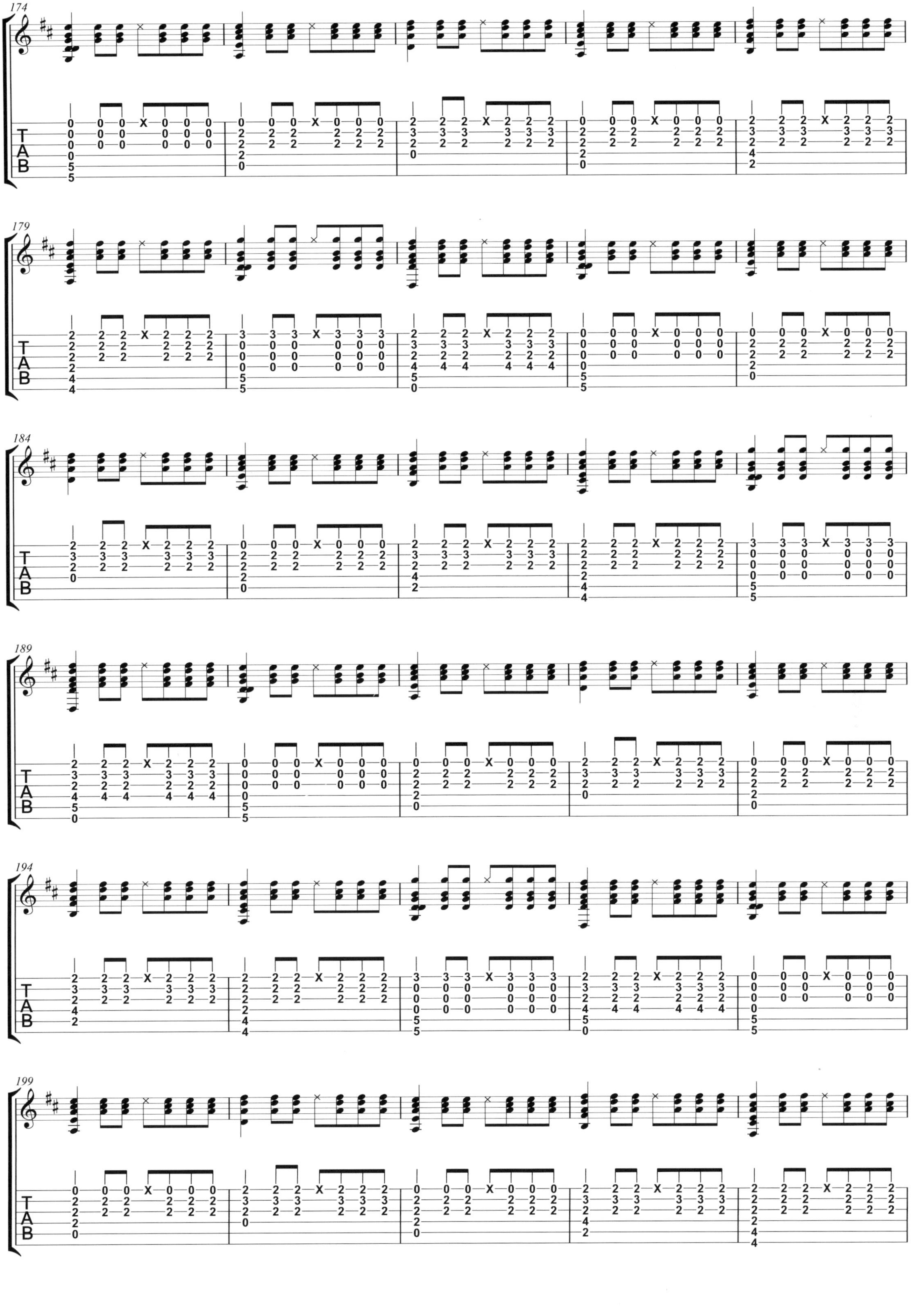
174
179
184
189
194
199
TAB

204
209
214
219
cresc.
cresc.
224
227
ff
ff
TAB

Guitar 3

Pachelbel's "Loose" Canon

arranged for four guitars
by The Los Angeles Guitar Quartet

Standard Notation and Tablature

1 2 3 4 5 6 7 8 9 0

Visit us on the Web at www.melbay.com — E-mail us at email@melbay.com

Standard Notation

Pachelbel's "Loose" Canon

Guitar 3

⑥ = D
⑦ = A (if using 7-string)

Johann Pachelbel (1653-1706)
"Loosely" arranged by the Los Angeles Guitar Quartet

Tumbao
=112
mf loco
CIII
f
Bluegrass
=112 slight swing feel
"country" strum like
banjo frailing pattern
p
mf

♩= 126
6
percussion ad lib: slap strings against frets, muted strings
Disco
♩= 94
Funk bass style
f
(8vb)
Jazz
♩= 168 swing
mp fleshy jazz double-bass sound

136
⑤
Grunge
143
♩= 120
2
⑥
ff
Pa-chel- bel!!
scream in grunge
guttural style
147
150
Rumba
♩=200+
tune ⑥ to E
23
(slap on strings w/palm)
mf
strum in rumba style
177
simile
181
185
189
194
200

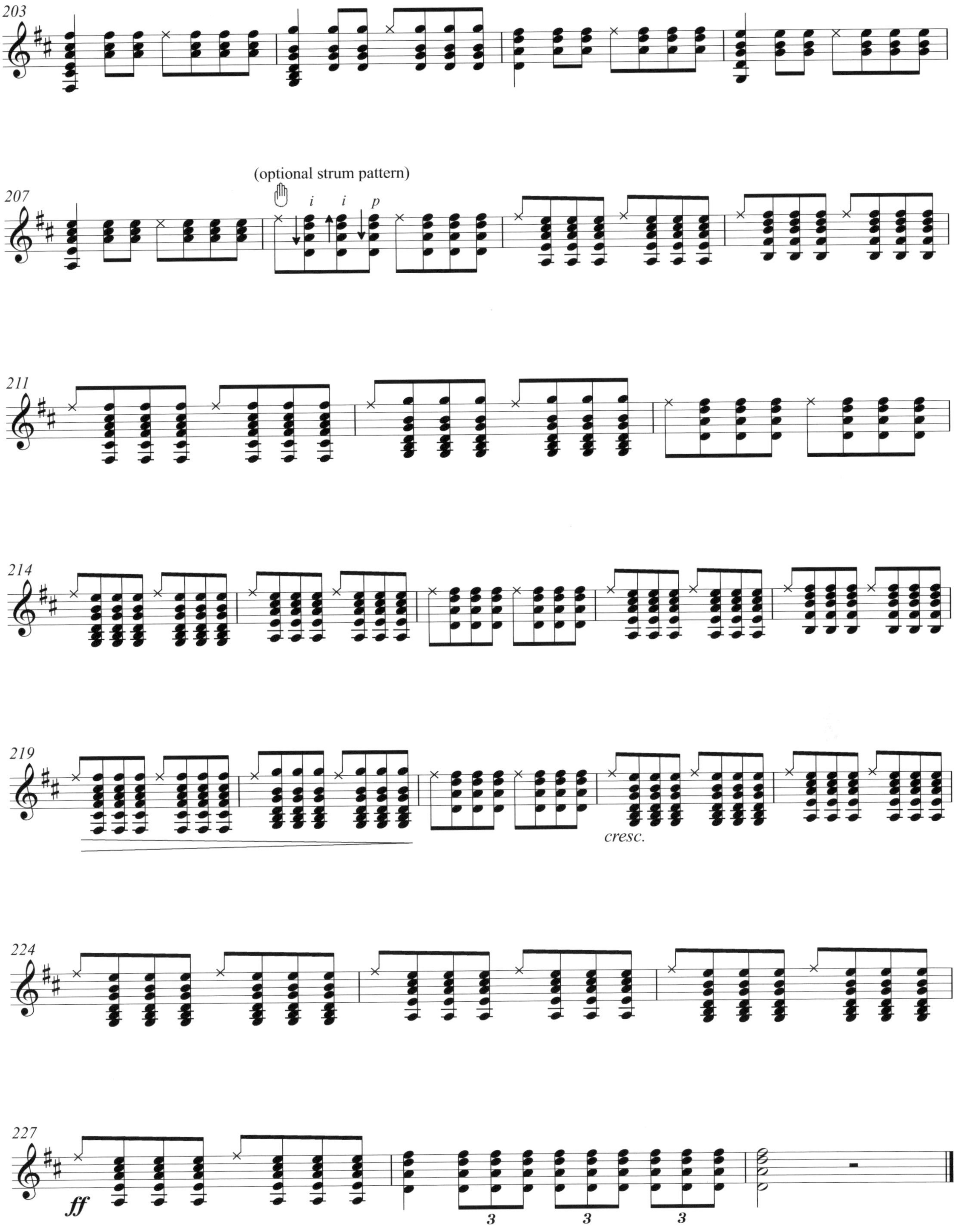
203
207
(optional strum pattern)
i i p
211
214
219
cresc.
224
227
ff
3 3 3

Tablature

Pachelbel's "Loose" Canon

Guitar 3

Johann Pachelbel (1653-1706)
"Loosely" arranged by the Los Angeles Guitar Quartet

⑥ = D
⑦ = A (if using 7-string)

Tumbao
♩=112
mf
loco
CIII

CIII
Bluegrass
=112 slight swing feel
"country" strum like
banjo frailing pattern

♩= 126
percussion ad lib: slap strings against frets, muted strings
Disco
♩= 94
Funk bass style
Funk bass style

(8vb)
Jazz
♩= 168 swing
mp fleshy jazz double-bass sound
Grunge
♩= 120
ff
Pa -chel - bel!!
scream in grunge guttural style
Pa-chel- bel!!
scream in grunge guttural style

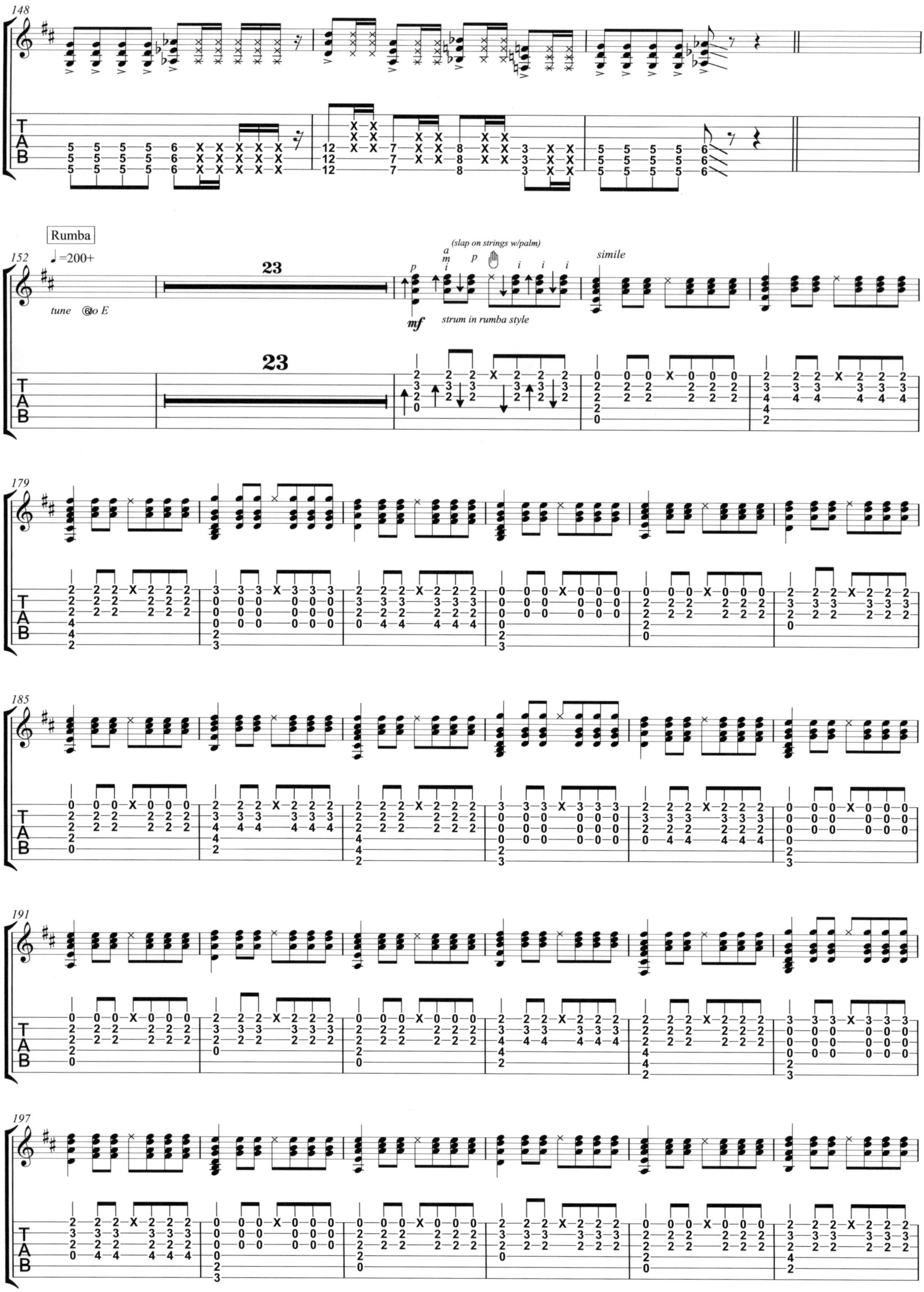
148
Rumba
152
♩=200+
tune ⑥ to E
23
(slap on strings w/palm)
mf
strum in rumba style
simile
179
185
191
197

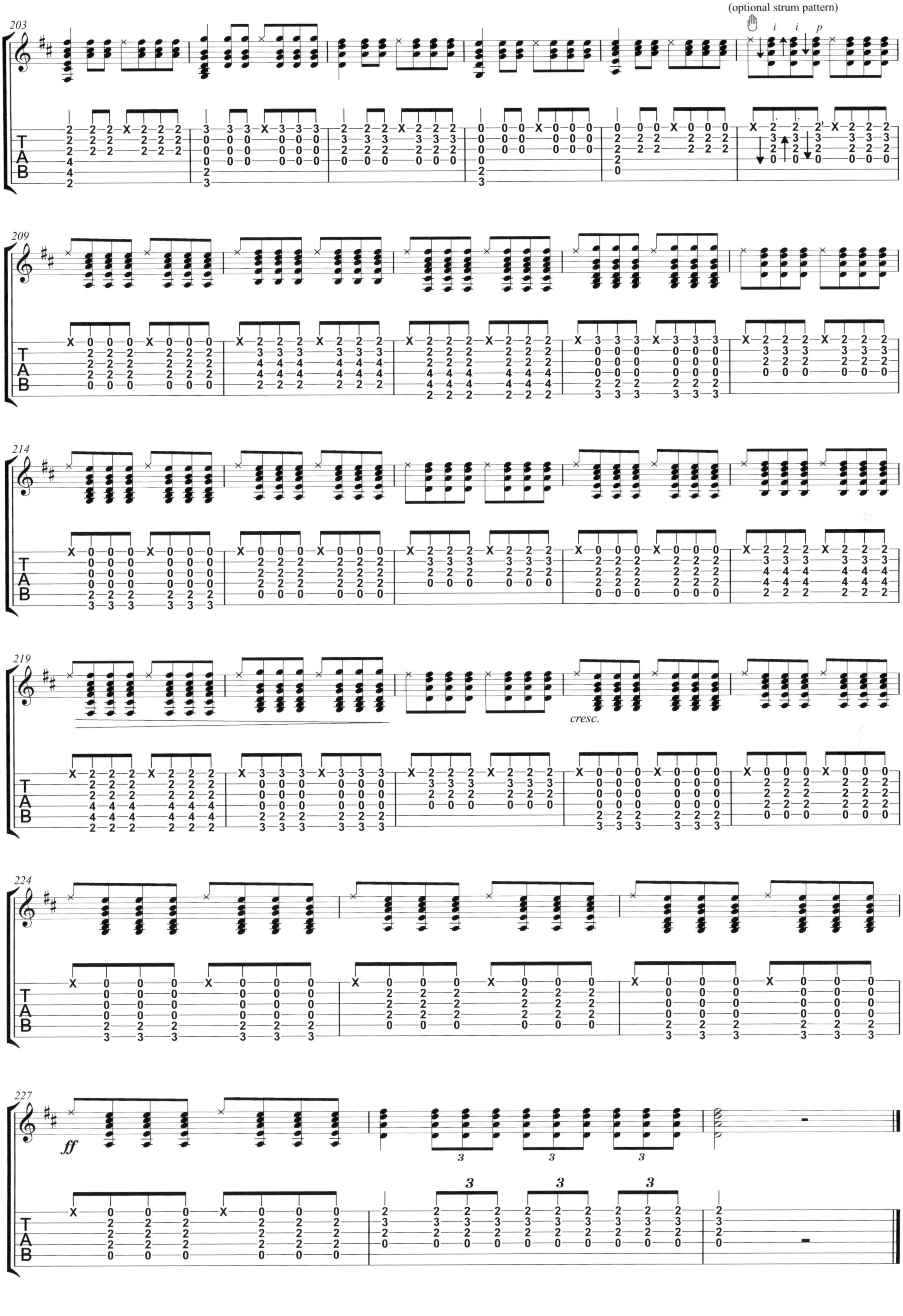
(optional strum pattern)
i i p
203
209
214
219
cresc.
224
227
ff
TAB

MEL BAY ®

Guitar 4

Pachelbel's "Loose" Canon

arranged for four guitars
by The Los Angeles Guitar Quartet

Standard Notation and Tablature

1 2 3 4 5 6 7 8 9 0

Visit us on the Web at www.melbay.com — E-mail us at email@melbay.com

Standard Notation

Pachelbel's "Loose Canon"

Guitar 4

Johann Pachelbel (1653-1706)
"Loosely" arranged by the Los Angeles Guitar Quartet

Bluegrass
𝅗𝅥=112 slight swing feel
bright and accented; w/plectrum if possible
♩= 126
quick strum
simile
Disco
♩= 94
Repeat 2 times
mf
funk strum ad lib.
choke
stroke

Jazz
♩ = 168 swing
Andy's solo
mf
Matt's optional solo; or improvise ad lib over changes
DMaj7 A7(b13) Bm9 F#7(b13)
GMaj7 A13(b9) A13(b9) GMaj6 A7(b13)
DMaj7 A7(b13) Fm7 Bb7(b13) GMaj7 A13(b9)
DMaj7 GMaj6 A7(b9) DMaj7
A7(b13) DMaj7 F#7(b13) GMaj7

DMaj7
GMaj6
A13(b9)
Grunge
♩ = 120
ff 8va
improvise wildly, using notes above fretboard
Pa-chel- bel!!
scream in grunge guttural style
continue to improvise freely and wildy, utilizing glisses
Rumba
♩ = 200+
molto staccato, sempre apoyando; "Gipsy Kings" style
a m i
f

193
198
203
208
214
220
cresc.
225
ff

Tablature

Pachelbel's "Loose" Canon

Guitar 4

Johann Pachelbel (1653-1706)
"Loosely" arranged by the Los Angeles Guitar Quartet

Bluegrass
𝅗𝅥=112 slight swing feel
bright and accented; w/plectrum if possible

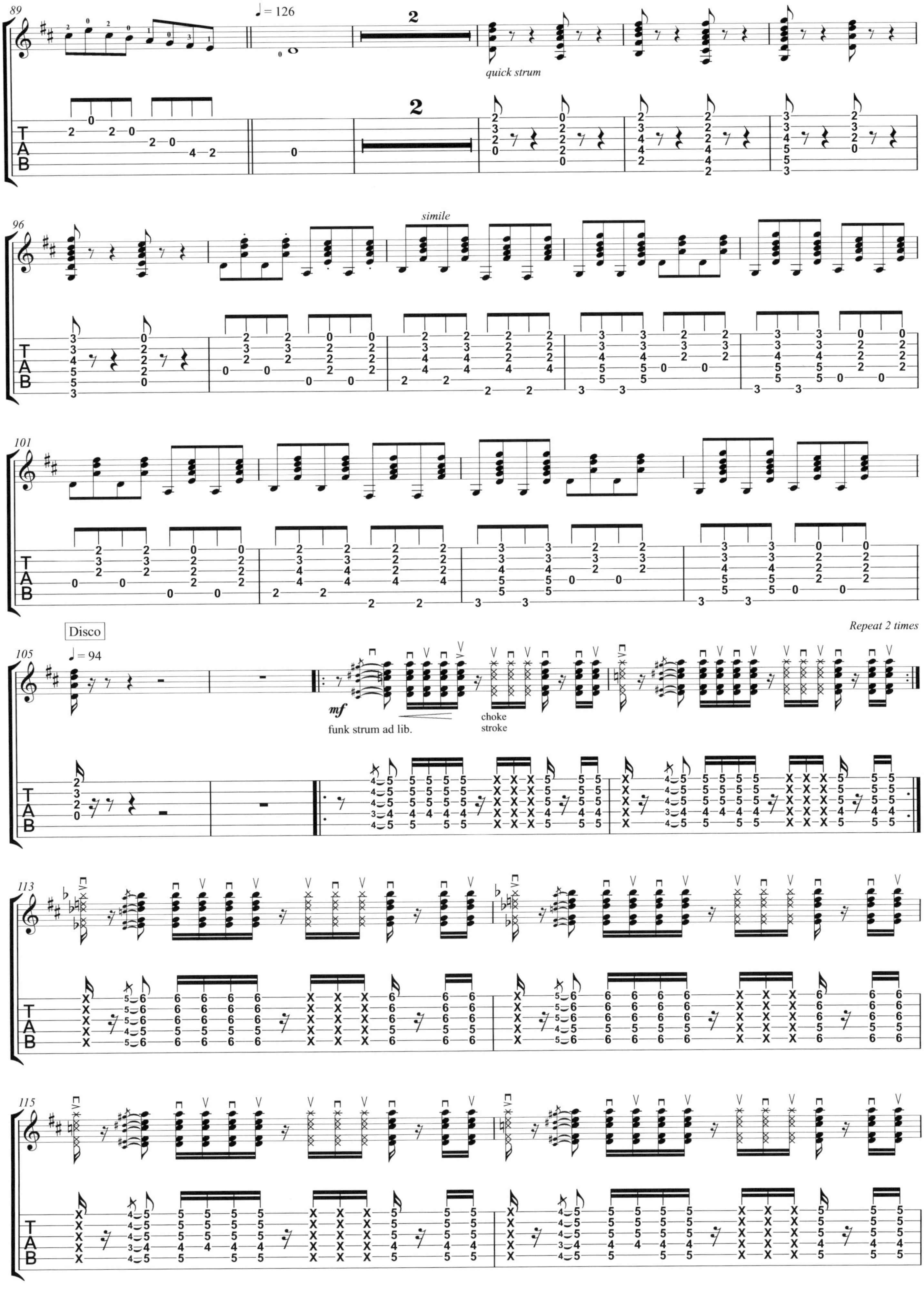

♩ = 126
quick strum
simile
Disco
♩ = 94
mf
funk strum ad lib.
choke stroke
Repeat 2 times

Jazz
♩= 168 swing
DMaj7
Andy's solo
mf
A7(b13)
Bm9
Guitar
Matt's optional solo; or improvise ad lib over changes
F#7(b13)
GMaj7
A13(b9)
GMaj6
Fm7
Bb7(b13)

DMaj7
GMaj6
A7(b9)
DMaj7
A7(b13)
DMaj7
F#7(b13)
GMaj7
DMaj7
GMaj6
A13(b9)
Grunge
♩= 120

Pa -chel - bel!!
ff 8va
scream in grunge guttural style
continue to improvise freely and wildly, utilizing glisses
improvise wildly, using notes above fretboard
Pa-chel- bel!!
scream in grunge guttural style
Rumba
♩= 200+
molto staccato, sempre apoyando; "Gipsy Kings" style
15
a m i
f

195
201
207
213
219
cresc.
225
ff
TAB

MEL BAY®